Table Of Contents

Chapter 1: Understanding Trauma and its Impact

Defining Trauma

Trauma is a word that is often thrown around casually in everyday conversations, but its true meaning and impact go much deeper. In the context of trauma-focused cognitive behavioral therapy (CBT) for adults, it is crucial to have a clear understanding of what trauma actually entails.

Trauma can be defined as any event or series of events that overwhelms an individual's ability to cope and leaves a lasting impact on their mental and emotional well-being. These events can range from natural disasters and accidents to physical, emotional, or sexual abuse. Trauma is unique to each individual, as what may be traumatic to one person may not be to another.

Trauma can result in a variety of symptoms, including flashbacks, nightmares, anxiety, depression, and difficulty forming relationships. It can also lead to maladaptive coping mechanisms such as substance abuse, self-harm, and avoidance of triggers.

In trauma-focused CBT, the goal is to help individuals process their traumatic experiences, challenge negative beliefs about themselves and the world, and develop healthier coping strategies. By addressing the root causes of their symptoms and working through their emotions in a safe and supportive environment, patients can reclaim their lives and move forward towards healing and growth.

It is important for adults seeking help for trauma to recognize that they are not defined by their past experiences. With the right support and tools, they can learn to navigate their trauma and build a brighter future for themselves.

Understanding the true nature of trauma is the first step towards reclaiming one's life.

Types of Trauma

In the journey of healing from trauma, it is important to understand the different types of trauma that one may have experienced. Trauma can come in many forms and can impact individuals in various ways. In this subchapter, we will explore some of the most common types of trauma that adults may have encountered.

One type of trauma is interpersonal trauma, which includes experiences such as physical, emotional, or sexual abuse, neglect, or betrayal by a trusted individual. These experiences can have a profound impact on a person's sense of safety and trust in others.

Another type of trauma is complex trauma, which involves exposure to multiple traumatic events over an extended period of time. This type of trauma can be particularly challenging to overcome, as it may have occurred in the context of ongoing abuse or neglect.

Additionally, there is also traumatic grief, which occurs when an individual experiences the sudden or unexpected loss of a loved one. This type of trauma can be overwhelming and may result in intense feelings of sadness, anger, and guilt.

Other types of trauma include natural disasters, accidents, medical trauma, and community violence. Each of these experiences can have a unique impact on an individual's mental and emotional well-being.

It is important for individuals to recognize the type of trauma they have experienced in order to effectively address and heal from it. By understanding the different types of trauma, individuals can begin to make sense of their experiences and work towards reclaiming their lives.

In the following chapters, we will explore how trauma-focused cognitive behavioral therapy (CBT) can be used to help adults heal from various types of trauma and move towards a healthier and more fulfilling life.

Effects of Trauma on Adults

Trauma can have a profound impact on adults, affecting every aspect of their lives. The effects of trauma can manifest in various ways, including physical, emotional, and psychological symptoms. Understanding how trauma impacts adults is crucial for those seeking to reclaim their lives and heal from past experiences.

One of the most common effects of trauma on adults is the development of mental health issues such as anxiety, depression, and post-traumatic stress disorder (PTSD). These conditions can be debilitating, making it difficult for individuals to cope with everyday stressors and maintain healthy relationships. Trauma can also lead to feelings of shame, guilt, and low self-esteem, further complicating the healing process.

In addition to mental health concerns, trauma can also have physical effects on adults. Chronic pain, fatigue, and other physical symptoms are common among trauma survivors. These physical manifestations of trauma can be challenging to manage and may require a multidisciplinary approach to treatment.

Furthermore, trauma can impact adults' relationships with others. Survivors of trauma may struggle to trust others, have difficulty forming and maintaining connections, and may experience challenges in intimate relationships. These relational difficulties can further isolate individuals and hinder their ability to heal and move forward.

Despite the profound effects of trauma on adults, it is possible to reclaim your life and find healing through trauma-focused cognitive behavioral therapy (CBT). This evidence-based approach can help individuals process their traumatic experiences, challenge negative thought patterns, and develop healthy coping strategies. By addressing the effects of trauma head-on, adults can begin to heal, rebuild their lives, and create a brighter future for themselves.

Common Symptoms of Trauma in Adults

Understanding the common symptoms of trauma in adults is crucial for anyone who has experienced a traumatic event. These symptoms can manifest in various ways and may impact every aspect of a person's life. By recognizing these symptoms, individuals can begin to address their trauma and work towards reclaiming their lives.

One of the most common symptoms of trauma in adults is re-experiencing the traumatic event through flashbacks, nightmares, or intrusive thoughts. These experiences can be overwhelming and may lead to feelings of fear, anxiety, and helplessness. Additionally, adults who have experienced trauma may avoid situations or people that remind them of the traumatic event, leading to feelings of isolation and disconnection from others.

Other common symptoms of trauma in adults include hypervigilance, irritability, difficulty concentrating, and sleep disturbances. These symptoms can make it challenging to engage in daily activities and may impact relationships with family, friends, and coworkers. Adults who have experienced trauma may also struggle with feelings of guilt, shame, and self-blame, leading to low self-esteem and self-worth.

It is essential for adults who have experienced trauma to seek support and professional help to address these symptoms. Trauma-focused cognitive-behavioral therapy (CBT) has been shown to be an effective treatment for trauma-related symptoms in adults. Through therapy, individuals can learn coping skills, process their trauma, and work towards reclaiming their lives.

If you are experiencing any of these symptoms, know that you are not alone. Reach out to a mental health professional who specializes in trauma-focused CBT for adults to begin your journey towards healing and reclaiming your life. Remember, healing is possible, and you deserve to live a life free from the grip of trauma.

Chapter 2: Introduction to Trauma-Focused Cognitive Behavioral Therapy (TF-CBT)

What is TF-CBT?

Principles of TF-CBT

In this subchapter, we will explore the key principles of Trauma-Focused Cognitive Behavioral Therapy (TF-CBT) and how they can help you reclaim your life after experiencing trauma. TF-CBT is a highly effective therapy approach that has been specifically designed for adults who have experienced traumatic events.

One of the core principles of TF-CBT is the importance of creating a safe and supportive therapeutic environment. Your therapist will work closely with you to build a trusting relationship and provide a space where you feel comfortable discussing your experiences and emotions. This safe environment is essential for the healing process to begin.

Another key principle of TF-CBT is the focus on understanding and processing the impact of trauma on your thoughts, feelings, and behaviors. Through guided exercises and discussions, you will learn how to identify and challenge negative beliefs that may have developed as a result of the trauma. By gaining insight into these patterns, you can begin to replace them with healthier ways of thinking and responding.

TF-CBT also emphasizes the importance of learning coping skills to manage distressing emotions and triggers. Your therapist will teach you techniques such as mindfulness, relaxation, and grounding exercises to help you regulate your emotions and stay present in the moment. These skills can be invaluable in helping you navigate difficult situations and reduce the impact of trauma on your daily life.

By embracing the principles of TF-CBT and working closely with your therapist, you can begin to reclaim your life and move forward from the pain of the past. Remember, healing from trauma is a journey, but with the right support and guidance, you can find hope and healing along the way.

How TF-CBT Works

Trauma-Focused Cognitive Behavioral Therapy (TF-CBT) is a highly effective treatment approach for adults who have experienced trauma. This therapy focuses on helping individuals process and cope with traumatic events in a safe and structured environment. TF-CBT is based on the understanding that trauma can have a significant impact on a person's thoughts, emotions, and behaviors, and that addressing these effects is essential for healing.

TF-CBT works by combining cognitive behavioral techniques with trauma-focused interventions to help individuals develop coping skills and process their traumatic experiences. The therapy typically involves several key components, including psychoeducation, relaxation techniques, cognitive restructuring, exposure therapy, and skills training.

During TF-CBT sessions, patients work with a trained therapist to identify and challenge negative thoughts and beliefs about themselves and their trauma. Through cognitive restructuring, individuals learn to replace these harmful thoughts with more realistic and adaptive beliefs. Exposure therapy may also be used to help patients confront and process their trauma in a safe and controlled manner, gradually reducing their fear and anxiety.

In addition to cognitive restructuring and exposure therapy, TF-CBT also focuses on building coping skills and resilience. Patients learn relaxation techniques to manage stress and anxiety, as well as interpersonal skills to improve relationships and communication. By developing these skills, individuals are better equipped to cope with the challenges of trauma and move forward in their healing journey.

Overall, TF-CBT offers a structured and evidence-based approach to trauma recovery for adults. By addressing the cognitive, emotional, and behavioral effects of trauma, this therapy empowers individuals to reclaim their lives and build a brighter future.

Benefits of TF-CBT for Adults

Trauma-Focused Cognitive Behavioral Therapy (TF-CBT) is a highly effective treatment approach for adults who have experienced trauma. This therapy is specifically designed to help individuals process and cope with traumatic experiences in a safe and structured manner. There are numerous benefits of TF-CBT for adults, making it a popular choice for those seeking to reclaim their lives after trauma.

One of the primary benefits of TF-CBT is that it provides a structured framework for processing traumatic experiences. This structured approach helps individuals to gradually confront and work through their trauma, allowing them to build coping skills and resilience along the way. By breaking down the trauma into manageable components, TF-CBT empowers adults to take control of their healing process and work towards recovery at their own pace.

Additionally, TF-CBT helps adults to develop a deeper understanding of their thoughts, emotions, and behaviors in relation to their trauma. Through techniques such as cognitive restructuring and mindfulness, individuals are able to challenge negative beliefs and develop healthier coping strategies. This increased self-awareness can lead to improved emotional regulation, reduced anxiety and depression, and an overall sense of empowerment.

TF-CBT also emphasizes the importance of building a strong support system and developing healthy relationships. By working with a trained therapist, adults can learn to communicate effectively, set boundaries, and establish trust in their relationships. This can help individuals to rebuild their sense of safety and security, ultimately leading to improved overall well-being.

Overall, TF-CBT offers adults a comprehensive and evidence-based approach to healing from trauma. By addressing the cognitive, emotional, and behavioral aspects of trauma, individuals can reclaim their lives and move forward with renewed hope and resilience.

Chapter 3: Getting Started with TF-CBT

Finding a Therapist

Finding a therapist who specializes in trauma-focused cognitive behavioral therapy (CBT) is an important step in reclaiming your life after experiencing trauma. There are several factors to consider when searching for the right therapist to help you on your healing journey.

First and foremost, it is essential to find a therapist who has experience working with adults who have experienced trauma. Look for a therapist who is trained in trauma-focused CBT specifically, as this type of therapy has been shown to be effective in helping individuals process and heal from traumatic experiences.

When searching for a therapist, consider asking for recommendations from trusted friends, family members, or healthcare providers. You can also search online for therapists in your area who specialize in trauma-focused CBT. Many therapists have websites where you can learn more about their background, experience, and treatment approach.

It is also important to consider factors such as location, cost, and availability when choosing a therapist. Make sure that the therapist's office is conveniently located and that their fees are within your budget. Additionally, consider whether the therapist offers evening or weekend appointments to accommodate your schedule.

Once you have found a therapist who meets your criteria, schedule an initial consultation to see if you feel comfortable and connected with them. Building a trusting relationship with your therapist is crucial for the success of your treatment. During the consultation, ask about the therapist's approach to trauma-focused CBT and how they plan to support you in your healing process.

Remember, finding the right therapist is a personal decision, and it may take time to find someone who is the right fit for you. Don't be afraid to ask questions and advocate for your needs as you search for a therapist who can help you reclaim your life after trauma.

Setting Goals for Therapy

Setting goals for therapy is an important step in the process of reclaiming your life after experiencing trauma. As adults seeking trauma-focused Cognitive Behavioral Therapy (CBT), it is crucial to have a clear understanding of what you hope to achieve through therapy and to communicate these goals effectively with your therapist.

When setting goals for therapy, it is helpful to start by reflecting on the challenges and difficulties you are currently facing as a result of the trauma you have experienced. This could include symptoms such as anxiety, depression, flashbacks, or difficulty trusting others. By identifying these challenges, you can begin to think about what specific changes you would like to see in your life as a result of therapy.

It is important to set realistic and achievable goals for therapy. While it is natural to want to see immediate and dramatic changes, healing from trauma is a gradual process that takes time and effort. By setting smaller, manageable goals, you can track your progress and celebrate your achievements along the way.

In addition to setting goals related to your symptoms and challenges, it can also be helpful to think about broader goals for therapy, such as building resilience, improving self-esteem, or strengthening relationships. These goals can provide a sense of direction and purpose as you work towards reclaiming your life and moving forward from the trauma you have experienced.

By setting clear and meaningful goals for therapy, you can create a roadmap for your healing journey and empower yourself to make positive changes in your life. Remember that you are not alone in this process, and your therapist is there to support you every step of the way.

Building Trust with Your Therapist

One of the most crucial aspects of therapy, especially when dealing with trauma, is the establishment of trust between you and your therapist. Building a strong and trusting relationship with your therapist is essential for effective treatment and healing. Here are some tips on how to build trust with your therapist:

1. Be open and honest: Trust is built on honesty and openness. It is important to share your thoughts, feelings, and experiences with your therapist, even if they are difficult or painful. Your therapist is there to help you navigate through these emotions and experiences in a safe and supportive environment.

2. Communicate your needs: It is important to communicate your needs and expectations to your therapist. Let them know what you hope to achieve from therapy and what support you require. A good therapist will listen to your needs and work with you to create a treatment plan that meets your goals.

3. Establish boundaries: Setting boundaries with your therapist is important for building trust. Let your therapist know what you are comfortable with and what you are not comfortable with. Respectful communication and mutual understanding of boundaries will help create a safe therapeutic relationship.

4. Give it time: Building trust takes time. It is normal to feel hesitant or unsure in the beginning stages of therapy. Give yourself and your therapist time to get to know each other and build a strong foundation of trust.

Remember, therapy is a collaborative process, and building trust with your therapist is essential for successful treatment. By being open, honest, and communicative, you can create a strong and supportive therapeutic relationship that will help you reclaim your life from trauma.

Creating a Safety Plan

One of the most crucial aspects of healing from trauma is creating a safety plan. This plan is designed to help you navigate difficult situations and cope with triggers that may arise. It is a proactive approach to managing your mental health and ensuring that you have the tools necessary to stay safe and healthy.

The first step in creating a safety plan is identifying your triggers. These are the situations, people, or places that may cause you distress or increase your anxiety. By recognizing these triggers, you can develop strategies to avoid or cope with them effectively.

Next, it is important to establish a support system. This may include trusted friends, family members, or mental health professionals who can provide assistance when you are feeling overwhelmed. Having a strong support network can make a significant difference in your ability to cope with trauma-related stress.

Additionally, it is essential to develop coping strategies that work for you. This may involve deep breathing exercises, mindfulness techniques, or engaging in activities that bring you joy and relaxation. Experiment with different coping mechanisms to find what works best for you.

Finally, make sure to have a crisis plan in place. This should include contact information for emergency services, as well as a list of people you can reach out to in case of a mental health crisis. Knowing that you have a plan in place can provide a sense of security and peace of mind.

Creating a safety plan is an essential part of the healing process for trauma survivors. By taking proactive steps to ensure your safety and well-being, you can reclaim your life and move forward with confidence and resilience.

Chapter 4: Cognitive Restructuring Techniques

Recognizing Negative Thought Patterns

In our journey to reclaiming our lives after trauma, one of the most important steps is to recognize and challenge negative thought patterns that may be holding us back. These thought patterns can often become ingrained in our minds after experiencing trauma, leading to feelings of self-doubt, worthlessness, and hopelessness. By identifying and addressing these negative thoughts, we can begin to take back control of our lives and move towards healing and recovery.

One common negative thought pattern that many individuals experience after trauma is catastrophizing. This involves imagining the worst possible outcomes in any given situation, leading to increased anxiety and fear. By recognizing when we are catastrophizing and challenging these thoughts with evidence-based reasoning, we can begin to reframe our thinking and approach situations with a more balanced perspective.

Another common negative thought pattern is black and white thinking, where individuals see things in extremes with no middle ground. This can lead to feelings of perfectionism and unrealistic expectations of ourselves and others. By learning to recognize when we are engaging in black and white thinking and practicing self-compassion and acceptance, we can begin to break free from this harmful pattern.

It is important for adults undergoing trauma-focused Cognitive Behavioral Therapy (CBT) to work with their therapists to identify and challenge these negative thought patterns. By developing self-awareness and mindfulness, individuals can begin to interrupt the cycle of negative thinking and replace it with more positive and adaptive thoughts. Through this process, patients can reclaim their lives and move towards a more fulfilling and empowered future.

Recognizing and challenging negative thought patterns is a crucial step in the journey towards healing and recovery after trauma. By taking the time to identify these patterns and work towards changing them, individuals can begin to break free from the grip of their past experiences and move towards a brighter and more hopeful future.

Challenging and Changing Negative Thoughts

In the journey of healing from trauma, one of the most important steps is challenging and changing negative thoughts. Negative thoughts can often become ingrained in our minds after experiencing a traumatic event, leading to feelings of fear, anxiety, and hopelessness. However, by actively working to challenge and change these negative thoughts, we can begin to reclaim our lives and move towards a place of healing and recovery.

One of the first steps in challenging negative thoughts is to become aware of them. Pay attention to the thoughts that pop into your mind throughout the day, especially when you are feeling anxious or upset. Once you have identified these negative thoughts, it is important to question their validity. Ask yourself if there is evidence to support these thoughts, or if they are simply a result of your trauma.

Next, work on replacing these negative thoughts with more positive and realistic ones. For example, if you catch yourself thinking "I am worthless," try replacing that thought with "I am worthy of love and respect." This can be a challenging process, but with practice, you can begin to retrain your brain to think in a more positive and empowering way.

It is also helpful to enlist the support of a therapist or support group to help you navigate this process. They can provide you with tools and techniques to challenge negative thoughts, as well as offer encouragement and guidance along the way.

By actively working to challenge and change negative thoughts, you can begin to take control of your healing journey and move towards a place of empowerment and resilience. Remember, you are not defined by your trauma, and you have the power to reclaim your life and create a brighter future for yourself.

Developing Positive Self-Talk

Developing Positive Self-Talk is a crucial aspect of the healing journey for adults who have experienced trauma. Trauma-focused Cognitive Behavioral Therapy (CBT) emphasizes the importance of changing negative thought patterns and beliefs that may have developed as a result of traumatic experiences. By learning to engage in positive self-talk, individuals can begin to challenge and reframe these harmful beliefs, ultimately reclaiming their lives from the grips of trauma.

One of the first steps in developing positive self-talk is becoming aware of the negative thoughts that arise in your mind. Pay attention to the messages you tell yourself and the language you use. Are you constantly putting yourself down or doubting your abilities? Once you have identified these negative thought patterns, you can start to challenge them by replacing them with more positive and empowering statements.

It can be helpful to create a list of affirmations or positive statements that you can repeat to yourself regularly. These affirmations should be personalized to address the specific areas where you struggle with self-doubt or negative self-talk. For example, if you often feel unworthy of love or success, you could repeat an affirmation such as, "I am deserving of love and happiness."

In addition to affirmations, practicing mindfulness can also help you become more aware of your thoughts and emotions. By staying present in the moment and observing your thoughts without judgment, you can begin to distance yourself from negative self-talk and cultivate a more compassionate inner dialogue.

Remember, developing positive self-talk is a process that takes time and practice. Be patient with yourself as you work to rewire your brain and replace negative beliefs with more empowering ones. With dedication and perseverance, you can reclaim your life from the effects of trauma and cultivate a more positive and resilient mindset.

Practicing Mindfulness

Practicing mindfulness is an essential component of trauma-focused Cognitive Behavioral Therapy (CBT) for adults. Mindfulness involves being fully present in the moment, acknowledging and accepting your thoughts, feelings, and sensations without judgment. By practicing mindfulness, individuals can develop greater self-awareness and emotional regulation skills, which are crucial for overcoming trauma-related symptoms.

One of the key benefits of mindfulness is its ability to help individuals stay grounded and centered, even when faced with triggers or distressing memories. By focusing on the present moment, rather than getting caught up in past traumas or future worries, patients can learn to manage their emotions more effectively and prevent themselves from becoming overwhelmed.

In the context of trauma-focused CBT, mindfulness can be used to help patients recognize and challenge negative thought patterns that may be contributing to their symptoms. By observing their thoughts without judgment, patients can begin to see how these thoughts are influencing their emotions and behaviors, and work towards developing more balanced and realistic perspectives.

Mindfulness practices such as deep breathing exercises, body scans, and guided meditations can also help patients cultivate a sense of calm and relaxation, which is especially important for individuals who may be experiencing heightened levels of stress or anxiety as a result of their trauma. By incorporating mindfulness into their daily routine, patients can begin to rewire their brains and create new neural pathways that support healing and recovery.

Overall, practicing mindfulness is a powerful tool for adults undergoing trauma-focused CBT, as it can help them develop greater self-awareness, emotional regulation, and resilience in the face of adversity. By committing to mindfulness practices, patients can reclaim their lives and move towards a brighter, more hopeful future.

Chapter 5: Exposure Therapy

Understanding Exposure Therapy

Exposure therapy is a key component of trauma-focused cognitive behavioral therapy (CBT) for adults. It is a proven and effective treatment approach that helps individuals confront and process traumatic events in a safe and controlled environment. Exposure therapy works by gradually exposing individuals to the memories, thoughts, and situations that trigger their traumatic reactions, allowing them to confront and overcome their fears.

In exposure therapy, patients work closely with a therapist to create a hierarchy of feared situations or memories related to their trauma. This hierarchy is used to gradually expose patients to these triggers in a systematic way, starting with less distressing situations and gradually progressing to more challenging ones. Through repeated exposure, patients learn to tolerate distressing thoughts and emotions associated with their trauma, ultimately reducing their fear and anxiety responses.

It is important for patients undergoing exposure therapy to understand that experiencing some level of discomfort or anxiety during the process is normal and expected. The goal of exposure therapy is not to eliminate all distress, but rather to help patients develop coping strategies and resilience in the face of their traumatic memories.

By engaging in exposure therapy, individuals can reclaim their lives from the grip of trauma and move towards healing and recovery. It is a gradual and empowering process that requires commitment and courage, but the benefits can be life-changing. If you are considering exposure therapy as part of your trauma-focused CBT treatment, remember that you are not alone. Your therapist will guide and support you every step of the way towards reclaiming your life from the effects of trauma.

Gradual Exposure Techniques

In the journey of reclaiming your life after experiencing trauma, gradual exposure techniques can be incredibly powerful tools to help you overcome fear and anxiety. Trauma-focused Cognitive Behavioral Therapy (CBT) for adults often incorporates these techniques to help patients gradually confront and process their traumatic experiences in a safe and controlled manner.

Gradual exposure involves facing your fears or triggers in a step-by-step fashion, starting with situations or memories that are less distressing and gradually working your way up to more challenging ones. This approach allows you to build confidence and resilience as you confront and process the difficult emotions associated with your trauma.

One of the key benefits of gradual exposure techniques is that they can help you reframe your thoughts and beliefs about the traumatic event. By facing your fears head-on, you can begin to challenge and change the negative beliefs that have been holding you back. Over time, you may find that the intensity of your emotional reactions diminishes, allowing you to regain a sense of control and empowerment over your life.

It's important to remember that gradual exposure should always be done under the guidance of a trained therapist who can provide support and guidance throughout the process. Your therapist will work with you to create a personalized exposure plan that fits your unique needs and goals.

As you engage in gradual exposure techniques, be gentle with yourself and remember that healing from trauma is a journey that takes time and patience. By facing your fears and working through your trauma in a structured and supportive environment, you can reclaim your life and move forward with confidence and resilience.

Managing Anxiety During Exposure

Exposure therapy is a key component of trauma-focused cognitive-behavioral therapy (CBT) for adults. It involves gradually exposing oneself to situations, memories, or thoughts that trigger anxiety in order to desensitize oneself to them. However, this can be a challenging process, as facing one's fears can evoke intense anxiety and distress.

One of the most important aspects of managing anxiety during exposure is to practice self-care and self-compassion. It is normal to feel anxious and uncomfortable when confronting traumatic memories or situations, and it is important to be gentle with yourself during this process. Remember that you are not alone in your struggles, and that it is okay to take breaks or seek support when needed.

Another helpful strategy for managing anxiety during exposure is to practice relaxation techniques. Deep breathing, progressive muscle relaxation, and mindfulness exercises can help calm your nervous system and reduce feelings of anxiety. Incorporating these techniques into your daily routine can help you cope with anxiety both during exposure sessions and in your everyday life.

It can also be helpful to challenge negative thoughts and beliefs that contribute to anxiety. Cognitive restructuring techniques can help you identify and challenge irrational beliefs that may be fueling your anxiety. By replacing negative thoughts with more realistic and balanced ones, you can reduce anxiety and increase your ability to cope with exposure.

Finally, remember to celebrate your successes, no matter how small they may seem. Each step you take towards facing your fears is a victory, and it is important to acknowledge and reward yourself for your bravery and resilience. With patience, self-care, and support, you can learn to manage anxiety during exposure and reclaim your life from the grip of trauma.

Processing Traumatic Memories

Processing traumatic memories is a crucial aspect of healing from past traumas. Trauma-focused Cognitive Behavioral Therapy (CBT) provides strategies and techniques to help individuals confront and process these difficult memories in a safe and therapeutic environment.

One of the first steps in processing traumatic memories is acknowledging and accepting the impact that the trauma has had on your life. This can be a challenging and emotional process, but it is an essential part of the healing journey. It is important to remember that it is okay to feel a range of emotions, including anger, sadness, and fear, as you work through these memories.

CBT techniques such as cognitive restructuring can help individuals challenge and change negative thought patterns that may be contributing to their distress. By reframing these thoughts and beliefs, individuals can begin to see their traumatic experiences in a new light and develop a more positive and empowered perspective.

Exposure therapy is another effective technique used in trauma-focused CBT to help individuals confront their traumatic memories in a controlled and safe manner. This involves gradually exposing oneself to the memories and triggers associated with the trauma, while learning coping strategies to manage the intense emotions that may arise.

It is important for individuals to work closely with a trained therapist during this process, as processing traumatic memories can be overwhelming and triggering. A therapist can provide guidance, support, and validation as individuals navigate through their past traumas and work towards reclaiming their lives.

Remember, processing traumatic memories is a brave and courageous step towards healing and reclaiming your life. With the right support and tools, you can learn to integrate these experiences into your story and move forward with strength and resilience.

Chapter 6: Building Coping Skills

Identifying Triggers

In order to reclaim your life and move forward from past traumas, it is crucial to identify the triggers that can cause distress and negative emotions. Triggers are stimuli that remind you of the traumatic event and can lead to feelings of anxiety, fear, or even panic. By recognizing these triggers, you can learn to manage your response and prevent them from controlling your life.

One of the first steps in identifying triggers is to pay attention to your thoughts, feelings, and physical sensations when you encounter a potentially triggering situation. Do you notice a sudden increase in heart rate? Are you feeling overwhelmed with emotions? These could be signs that you are being triggered.

It is also important to consider the context in which the trigger occurs. For example, certain places, people, or activities may remind you of the traumatic event and serve as triggers. By understanding the specific circumstances that lead to your distress, you can better prepare yourself to cope with them in the future.

Another helpful strategy for identifying triggers is to keep a journal of your experiences. Write down any situations that cause you to feel anxious or upset, as well as the thoughts and emotions that accompany them. This can help you track patterns and gain insight into what triggers your distress.

Once you have identified your triggers, it is important to develop coping strategies to manage them. This may involve practicing relaxation techniques, engaging in activities that bring you joy, or seeking support from a therapist or support group. By taking proactive steps to address your triggers, you can empower yourself to reclaim your life and move forward from past traumas.

Remember, identifying triggers is a crucial step in the healing process. By recognizing and addressing the stimuli that cause distress, you can take control of your emotional well-being and work towards a brighter future.

Developing Healthy Coping Strategies

In the journey of healing from trauma, developing healthy coping strategies is essential. Coping strategies are the tools we use to manage difficult emotions, thoughts, and situations that arise as a result of the trauma we have experienced. These strategies can help us navigate the challenges of daily life and work towards reclaiming our sense of well-being.

One key aspect of developing healthy coping strategies is self-awareness. Take the time to reflect on your current coping mechanisms and evaluate whether they are helping or hindering your progress. Are you turning to unhealthy behaviors such as substance abuse or self-harm to cope with your trauma? If so, it may be time to explore healthier alternatives.

One effective coping strategy is mindfulness. Mindfulness involves focusing on the present moment without judgment. This practice can help you become more aware of your thoughts and feelings, allowing you to respond to them in a more constructive way. Mindfulness techniques such as deep breathing exercises or guided meditations can be powerful tools for managing anxiety and stress.

Another important coping strategy is building a strong support system. Surround yourself with people who understand and validate your experiences. Seeking out therapy or support groups can provide a safe space to share your feelings and receive guidance from others who have been through similar traumas.

It's also crucial to engage in self-care activities that nourish your mind, body, and spirit. This could include exercise, hobbies, spending time in nature, or practicing relaxation techniques. Taking care of yourself is not selfish – it's necessary for your healing and well-being.

By developing healthy coping strategies, you can empower yourself to face the challenges of trauma recovery with resilience and strength. Remember, healing is a journey, and it's okay to seek help along the way. You deserve to reclaim your life and find peace after trauma.

Self-Soothing Techniques

In the journey of healing from trauma, it is essential to learn how to self-soothe during moments of distress or overwhelming emotions. Self-soothing techniques are valuable tools that can help adults cope with the difficulties that arise from past traumatic experiences. By practicing these techniques regularly, individuals can cultivate a sense of calm and inner peace amidst the chaos that trauma can bring.

One effective self-soothing technique is deep breathing. Taking slow, deep breaths can help regulate the body's stress response and bring a sense of relaxation. By focusing on the breath and slowing down the pace of inhaling and exhaling, individuals can calm their nervous system and ground themselves in the present moment.

Another helpful technique is progressive muscle relaxation. This involves tensing and then releasing different muscle groups in the body, starting from the toes and working up to the head. By systematically relaxing each muscle group, individuals can release physical tension and promote a sense of relaxation throughout the body.

Engaging in activities that bring joy and comfort can also be a powerful form of self-soothing. This could include listening to music, spending time in nature, or engaging in a creative outlet like painting or writing. Finding moments of pleasure and connection can help individuals feel more grounded and resilient in the face of trauma.

Ultimately, self-soothing techniques are about creating a toolbox of strategies that can be used to navigate the challenges of trauma. By incorporating these techniques into daily life, adults can reclaim their sense of agency and empowerment in the journey towards healing. Remember, self-care is not selfish – it is a necessary part of the healing process.

Creating a Support System

One of the most important aspects of healing from trauma is establishing a strong support system. This network of friends, family, therapists, and other professionals can provide the necessary emotional, physical, and mental support needed to navigate the challenges of recovery. In this chapter, we will explore the importance of creating a support system and provide practical tips for building one that meets your unique needs.

First and foremost, it is crucial to identify individuals in your life who can be part of your support system. This may include trusted friends or family members who have shown empathy and understanding towards your trauma. It may also involve seeking out therapists or support groups that specialize in trauma-focused cognitive behavioral therapy (CBT) for adults. These professionals can offer specialized guidance and techniques to help you work through your trauma in a safe and structured manner.

Once you have identified potential support system members, it is important to communicate your needs and boundaries clearly. Let them know how they can best support you, whether it be through active listening, providing practical assistance, or simply being present during difficult times. Establishing clear boundaries will help ensure that your relationships remain healthy and supportive throughout your recovery process.

In addition to personal relationships, it can also be helpful to engage in self-care activities that promote emotional well-being. This may include practicing mindfulness, engaging in regular exercise, or pursuing hobbies that bring you joy and relaxation. Taking care of yourself is essential to building a strong support system, as it allows you to show up fully for yourself and others.

By creating a support system that meets your unique needs and boundaries, you can feel empowered to reclaim your life and heal from trauma. Remember that you are not alone in this journey, and that there are people and resources available to help you every step of the way.

Chapter 7: Maintaining Progress and Preventing Relapse

Recognizing Warning Signs of Relapse

Recognizing warning signs of relapse is crucial in maintaining progress and preventing setbacks in your recovery journey. In the book "Reclaiming Your Life: Trauma Focused CBT for Adults," we aim to help adults who have experienced trauma understand and identify these warning signs to take proactive steps towards maintaining their mental well-being.

One of the key warning signs of relapse is a sudden change in mood or behavior. This could manifest as increased irritability, withdrawal from social activities, or feelings of hopelessness and despair. It is important to pay attention to these shifts and reach out for support when needed.

Another warning sign to watch out for is an increase in substance use or other harmful coping mechanisms. Turning to alcohol, drugs, or other destructive behaviors to numb pain or avoid facing difficult emotions can be a sign that you are struggling to cope with your trauma. Seeking professional help and finding healthier ways to manage stress is essential in preventing relapse.

Additionally, physical symptoms such as trouble sleeping, changes in appetite, or unexplained aches and pains can also indicate that you are at risk of relapse. These symptoms are often linked to increased levels of stress and anxiety, which can exacerbate trauma-related symptoms.

By recognizing these warning signs early on, you can take proactive steps to prevent relapse and continue on your path to healing. Remember that reaching out for help is a sign of strength, not weakness, and there are resources available to support you in your recovery journey. Stay vigilant, prioritize self-care, and know that you are not alone in this process.

Building Resilience

Building resilience is an essential component of the healing journey for individuals who have experienced trauma. Resilience is the ability to adapt and bounce back from difficult experiences, and it is a skill that can be developed and strengthened over time.

In the context of trauma-focused cognitive behavioral therapy (CBT) for adults, building resilience involves learning how to cope with the emotional and psychological effects of trauma in a healthy and constructive way. This may include developing coping strategies, setting boundaries, and learning how to regulate emotions.

One important aspect of building resilience is developing a support network. Connecting with others who have experienced trauma can help individuals feel less alone and more understood. Building relationships with supportive friends, family members, or therapists can provide a sense of safety and security that is essential for healing.

Another key component of building resilience is developing self-care practices. Taking care of the body and mind through activities such as exercise, meditation, and healthy eating can help individuals feel more grounded and resilient in the face of adversity.

It is also important for individuals to challenge negative thought patterns and beliefs that may be holding them back. Through CBT techniques such as cognitive restructuring, individuals can learn to identify and challenge unhelpful thoughts, leading to a more positive and resilient mindset.

Overall, building resilience is a crucial part of the healing process for individuals who have experienced trauma. By developing coping strategies, building a support network, practicing self-care, and challenging negative thought patterns, individuals can strengthen their ability to bounce back from difficult experiences and reclaim their lives.

Continuing Self-Care Practices

In this subchapter, we will delve deeper into the importance of continuing self-care practices as part of your journey towards reclaiming your life after trauma. Self-care is not just a one-time activity; it is a lifelong commitment to your well-being and mental health. Trauma-focused Cognitive Behavioral Therapy (CBT) can be incredibly beneficial in helping you process and heal from past traumas, but it is equally important to incorporate ongoing self-care practices into your daily routine.

Self-care looks different for everyone, so it is essential to explore what works best for you. This could include activities such as mindfulness meditation, yoga, journaling, exercise, spending time in nature, or connecting with loved ones. The key is to find activities that help you relax, recharge, and nurture your mind, body, and spirit.

As you continue your journey towards healing, it can be easy to neglect self-care practices in favor of focusing solely on therapy. However, prioritizing self-care is crucial in maintaining your progress and preventing burnout. Remember, self-care is not selfish; it is a necessary part of your healing process.

Incorporating self-care practices into your daily routine can help you manage stress, reduce anxiety, and improve your overall well-being. By taking the time to care for yourself, you are investing in your mental health and building resilience in the face of future challenges.

So, as you continue your work in trauma-focused CBT, remember to make self-care a priority. Your journey towards reclaiming your life is a marathon, not a sprint, and practicing self-care along the way will ensure that you have the strength and resilience to face whatever comes your way.

Seeking Help When Needed

In the journey of healing from trauma, it is crucial to recognize when you need help and to have the courage to seek it. Seeking help when needed is not a sign of weakness, but rather a sign of strength and self-awareness. As adults, patients undergoing trauma focused CBT, it is important to understand that you do not have to face your struggles alone.

Therapy can be a safe and supportive space where you can explore your thoughts, feelings, and experiences in a non-judgmental environment. A trained therapist can provide you with tools and techniques to help you cope with the effects of trauma and work towards reclaiming your life.

It is common to feel hesitant or even ashamed about seeking help, but it is important to remember that therapy is a valuable resource that can help you heal and grow. Whether you are struggling with flashbacks, anxiety, depression, or any other symptom of trauma, therapy can provide you with the guidance and support you need to navigate through these challenges.

Remember that you deserve to live a fulfilling and meaningful life, free from the chains of past trauma. By seeking help when needed, you are taking a powerful step towards reclaiming your life and creating a brighter future for yourself. So, do not hesitate to reach out to a therapist or mental health professional who can support you on your journey towards healing and recovery. You are not alone, and there is hope for a better tomorrow.

Chapter 8: Embracing Your Healing Journey

Celebrating Milestones

In the journey of healing from trauma, it is important to acknowledge and celebrate the milestones along the way. These milestones serve as markers of progress and can help you stay motivated and hopeful as you continue on your path to reclaiming your life.

As adults who have experienced trauma, it can be easy to get caught up in the day-to-day challenges and struggles. However, taking the time to recognize and celebrate the progress you have made is essential for your mental and emotional well-being.

Milestones can come in many forms, whether it is completing a therapy session, facing a triggering situation, or simply getting through a difficult day. Each milestone is a testament to your strength and resilience in the face of adversity.

When celebrating milestones, it is important to reflect on how far you have come and the obstacles you have overcome. This can help you build confidence in your ability to cope with future challenges and setbacks.

One way to celebrate milestones is to treat yourself to something special, whether it is a small indulgence like a favorite dessert or a larger reward like a weekend getaway. By acknowledging your achievements in this way, you are reinforcing positive behaviors and self-care practices.

Another way to celebrate milestones is to share your successes with others. This could be with a trusted friend, family member, or therapist who can offer support and encouragement. Celebrating milestones with others can also help you feel connected and validated in your progress.

Overall, celebrating milestones is an important part of the healing process. By recognizing and honoring your achievements, you are taking an active role in reclaiming your life from the impact of trauma. So take the time to celebrate your successes, no matter how small they may seem, and continue on your journey towards healing and recovery.

Reflecting on Your Growth

In this subchapter, we will explore the importance of reflecting on your growth throughout the journey of trauma-focused CBT. As adults and patients undergoing therapy, it is crucial to take the time to acknowledge and celebrate the progress you have made.

Reflecting on your growth can provide valuable insights into how far you have come since starting therapy. It allows you to recognize the changes you have made, both big and small, and appreciate the hard work you have put in to overcome the challenges you have faced.

Moreover, reflecting on your growth can help boost your self-esteem and confidence. By recognizing your achievements, you can build a sense of pride in yourself and your abilities to overcome adversity. This can be particularly empowering for individuals who have experienced trauma and may struggle with feelings of worthlessness or inadequacy.

Taking the time to reflect on your growth can also serve as a reminder of your resilience and strength. It can help you see that despite the difficulties you have faced, you have the capacity to heal and grow. This can be a powerful motivator to continue working towards your goals and building a positive future for yourself.

As you reflect on your growth, remember to be gentle with yourself. Healing from trauma is a complex process that takes time, patience, and effort. Celebrate the progress you have made, no matter how small, and continue to move forward with compassion and determination.

In conclusion, reflecting on your growth is an essential part of the therapy process. It can help you recognize your achievements, boost your self-esteem, and remind you of your resilience. Take the time to acknowledge how far you have come and use that knowledge to propel yourself further on your journey to reclaiming your life.

Setting Future Goals

Setting future goals is an essential part of the healing process in trauma-focused cognitive behavioral therapy (CBT) for adults. As you work through your past traumas and learn coping mechanisms, it is important to look towards the future and set goals for yourself. These goals can help you stay motivated, focused, and optimistic about the progress you are making in your therapy.

When setting future goals, it is important to be realistic and specific. Think about what you want to achieve in the short term and long term, both personally and professionally. Maybe you want to improve your relationships, pursue a new career path, or simply feel more at peace with yourself. Whatever your goals may be, make sure they are achievable and measurable so you can track your progress along the way.

It can also be helpful to break down your goals into smaller, more manageable steps. This can prevent you from feeling overwhelmed and make it easier to stay on track. For example, if your goal is to improve your mental health, you could set smaller goals such as practicing mindfulness daily, attending therapy sessions regularly, or reaching out to a support group for help.

Remember, setting future goals is not about perfection or achieving everything at once. It is about setting a direction for yourself and taking small steps towards a brighter future. Be patient with yourself, celebrate your successes, and learn from your setbacks. By setting future goals in trauma-focused CBT, you are reclaiming your life and taking control of your own healing journey.

Finding Meaning and Purpose in Life

Finding meaning and purpose in life is a crucial aspect of healing from trauma and reclaiming your life. Trauma can leave us feeling lost, disconnected, and unsure of our place in the world. However, by exploring what gives our lives meaning and purpose, we can begin to rebuild a sense of identity and move forward in a positive direction.

One way to find meaning and purpose in life is to reflect on your values and beliefs. What is important to you? What do you care about? By aligning your actions with your values, you can create a sense of purpose that guides your decisions and gives your life direction.

Another strategy is to set goals for yourself. By establishing clear, achievable goals, you can create a roadmap for your future and a sense of accomplishment as you work towards them. These goals can be big or small, but they should be meaningful to you and help you move towards the life you want to live.

Connecting with others can also help you find meaning and purpose in life. Building relationships with supportive friends, family members, or a therapist can provide a sense of belonging and connection that is essential for healing from trauma. By sharing your experiences and learning from others, you can gain new perspectives and insights that can help you navigate your own journey towards healing.

Ultimately, finding meaning and purpose in life is a deeply personal process that requires self-reflection, exploration, and a willingness to take risks. By engaging in this process, you can begin to reclaim your life and move towards a brighter, more fulfilling future.

Chapter 9: Conclusion - Living a Life Reclaimed

Reviewing Your Progress

As you continue on your journey of healing through trauma-focused cognitive behavioral therapy (CBT), it is important to take the time to reflect on your progress. This subchapter will guide you through the process of reviewing your progress, celebrating your achievements, and identifying areas for further growth.

One of the key aspects of trauma-focused CBT is the emphasis on monitoring and evaluating your progress throughout the therapeutic process. By regularly assessing how you are feeling, what strategies are working for you, and what challenges you are facing, you can make informed decisions about your treatment plan and adjust as needed.

Take a moment to reflect on how far you have come since starting therapy. Consider the goals you set for yourself at the beginning of treatment and how you have worked towards achieving them. Celebrate the small victories and milestones along the way, as they are signs of your resilience and progress.

In addition to looking back on your accomplishments, it is important to also acknowledge any setbacks or challenges you may have faced. These moments are opportunities for learning and growth, and can provide valuable insights into areas that may need additional attention or support.

Moving forward, consider setting new goals for yourself based on your current needs and priorities. Discuss these goals with your therapist and work together to develop a plan for achieving them. Remember that healing from trauma is a gradual process, and it is okay to take small steps towards your goals.

By regularly reviewing your progress, celebrating your achievements, and setting new goals, you can stay motivated and focused on reclaiming your life from the impact of trauma. Trust in yourself and the therapeutic process, and remember that you are deserving of healing and growth.

Embracing Your Strengths

In the journey of healing from trauma, it is essential to recognize and embrace your strengths. Trauma can often leave individuals feeling powerless and overwhelmed, but by acknowledging the unique qualities and abilities that you possess, you can begin to build a solid foundation for your recovery.

One of the first steps in embracing your strengths is to identify them. Take some time to reflect on the qualities that have helped you navigate difficult situations in the past. Perhaps you are resilient, compassionate, or resourceful. These strengths can serve as pillars of support as you work through the challenges of trauma recovery.

It is also important to recognize that everyone has strengths, even if they may not always be readily apparent. Sometimes, our strengths can be hidden beneath layers of self-doubt or negative beliefs. Through therapy and self-reflection, you can uncover these hidden strengths and learn to harness them to build a more fulfilling and empowered life.

As you begin to embrace your strengths, remember to practice self-compassion. Healing from trauma is a process that takes time and effort, and it is okay to have setbacks along the way. By treating yourself with kindness and understanding, you can create a safe space for growth and transformation.

By embracing your strengths, you are taking an active role in reclaiming your life from the grip of trauma. You have the power to shape your own narrative and create a future filled with hope and possibility. Trust in your abilities, lean on your strengths, and know that you are worthy of healing and happiness.

Moving Forward with Confidence

Now that you have completed the initial stages of trauma-focused CBT and have begun to process and make sense of your past experiences, it is time to focus on moving forward with confidence. This phase of therapy is all about building on the progress you have made and equipping yourself with the tools and strategies you need to navigate the challenges that lie ahead.

One of the key aspects of moving forward with confidence is developing a strong sense of self-compassion. Many trauma survivors struggle with feelings of shame, guilt, and self-blame, which can undermine their confidence and self-esteem. By practicing self-compassion, you can learn to treat yourself with kindness and understanding, even in the face of setbacks or challenges.

Another important aspect of moving forward with confidence is setting realistic goals for yourself. These goals should be specific, measurable, achievable, relevant, and time-bound (SMART), and should reflect your values and priorities. By setting goals that are meaningful to you and breaking them down into manageable steps, you can build a sense of accomplishment and momentum as you work towards them.

It is also important to cultivate a support network of friends, family members, or other trusted individuals who can provide encouragement, validation, and practical assistance as you continue your healing journey. Connecting with others who have shared similar experiences can also be valuable, as it can help you feel less alone and more understood.

By practicing self-compassion, setting realistic goals, and building a support network, you can move forward with confidence and continue to reclaim your life from the impact of trauma. Remember, healing is a journey, and it is okay to take it one step at a time. You have already shown great strength and resilience in seeking help and working through your trauma – now it is time to harness that strength and keep moving forward towards a brighter future.

Continuing Your Journey of Healing and Growth

Congratulations on completing the initial stages of trauma-focused CBT! You have taken a courageous step towards reclaiming your life and healing from past trauma. However, the journey does not end here. In fact, it is just the beginning of a lifelong process of healing and growth.

As you continue on your journey, it is important to remember that healing is not a linear process. There will be good days and bad days, progress and setbacks. Be gentle with yourself and give yourself the grace to navigate through the ups and downs of healing.

One key aspect of continuing your journey of healing and growth is to practice self-care. Take care of your physical, emotional, and mental well-being. Prioritize activities that bring you joy and peace, whether it's spending time in nature, practicing mindfulness, or engaging in creative outlets.

Another important aspect is to maintain a strong support system. Surround yourself with people who uplift and support you on your journey. Seek therapy or counseling if needed, to continue processing and working through your trauma.

Set realistic goals for yourself and celebrate your progress, no matter how small. Remember that healing is a marathon, not a sprint. Be patient with yourself and trust in your ability to continue growing and evolving.

Above all, continue to be kind and compassionate towards yourself. You deserve healing and happiness. Embrace the journey ahead with courage and resilience, knowing that you have the strength within you to reclaim your life and thrive. You are not alone on this journey – we are here to support you every step of the way.

Made in the USA
Las Vegas, NV
05 May 2024

89563184R00026